MUSIC

D0127109

COMMUNICATION
TODAY & TOMORROW

LIBRARY OF CONGRESS CATALOGING-IN-PUBLICATION DATA

Balcziak, Bill, 1962-
  Music / by Bill Balcziak.
    p. cm. -- (Communication)
  Includes index.
  ISBN 0-86592-056-7
  1. Sound--recording and reproducing. I. Title. II. Series: Communication
(Vero Beach, Fla.)
ML1055.B15 1989
621.389'32--dc20   89-6328
                                                                   CIP
                                                                   AC MN

MUSIC

TEXT BY
BILL BALCZIAK

DESIGN & PRODUCTION BY
MARK E. AHLSTROM
(The Bookworks)

**ROURKE
ENTERPRISES,
INC.**
Vero Beach, FL 32964
U.S.A.

MUSIC

TABLE OF CONTENTS

CREDITS

ILLUSTRATIONS:

Jeff Heger/FPG .... cover photo, 4
AP/Wide World Photos 7, 9, 15,
.... 17, 18, 20, 36
The Bettmann Archive 11, 13
FPG International 19, 34
Craig Roesler 23
D. Luria/FPG 24
M. Keller/FPG 27
J. Leung/FPG 29, 41
Gary Jochim/FPG 31
James E. Arconati/FPG 39
S. Mirabello/FPG 43

TYPESETTING AND LAYOUT: THE FINAL WORD
PRINTING: WORZALLA PUBLISHING CO.

It is late 1877. A group of important-looking businessmen and investors has gathered in a conference room in a Boston hotel. They are fascinated by an odd device on the table in front of them—the first phonograph.

The device looks like an old soup can that has been attached to a flat board by two posts. A grooved rod runs through the middle of it. At one end of the rod is a crank. And along one side rests a metal disc that looks like a candle holder lying on its side.

"Hah!" exclaims a stocky man between puffs on his cigar. "That Edison has gone crazy this time!" Around the room, heads nod in agreement. But from a dark corner of the room comes a polite voice. "I beg to differ," says a slight man in a pin-striped suit.

He steps close to the table and leans down to examine the machine. Looking back at the men, he says,

"Edison is a sharp fellow. Let's give him a chance!"

With that, 30-year-old inventor Thomas Edison steps briskly into the room. A few of the men say "hello," but he doesn't even turn his head. Thomas Edison is almost totally deaf.

Quietly, Edison leans over the machine. He begins turning the crank, slowly and steadily. The "tin can" makes a scratching noise, but this doesn't impress the men at all. Some of them cough impatiently. Others frown and shake their heads.

Suddenly a man's voice fills the room. The onlookers' heads jerk up. "What in tarnation is that?" cries the stocky man with the cigar. Edison smiles and gestures proudly toward his invention.

Finally the men understand. Some of them gasp in surprise. Others step back in shock. The sound is coming from Edison's invention. What an

Thomas Edison's phonograph surprised the world in 1877. Even though Edison was almost totally deaf, he saw the need for a machine that could "make noise."

amazing thing! The men have never seen—or heard—anything like this before.

Edison—called "The Wizard of Menlo Park"—has done the impossible once more. For the first time, sound can be recorded and then played back again—on a device no bigger than a hat box.

The man in the pin-striped suit bows to the inventor and smiles broadly. "Mr. Edison," he says, "this is the start of something big!"

It certainly was.

CHAPTER ONE

THE FIRST RECORDINGS

The Phonoautograph

Edison wasn't the first man who wanted to produce and record sound. History shows that people have been using mechanical devices to play music for thousands of years. Despite their attempts to explore sound and to refine music-making devices, the idea of recording sound was never more than a dream—until a little more than 100 years ago, that is.

In 1857, a man named Léon Scott built a device called the Phonoautograph. This crude—but clever—machine was the basis for Edison's phonograph. Scott's Phonoautograph could make a simple recording by tracing the movements of a stylus in response to sound. The stylus acted like the "needle" of a modern record player.

The Phonoautograph had one major drawback. Although it could record sound, it couldn't play it back! Yet the Phonoautograph proved to be a useful idea. The design is still used today in the making of recording thermometers and barometers.

The Phonograph

Edison was inspired by Scott's machine, but he wanted to improve on the idea. Even though he was almost totally deaf, he saw the need for a machine that could "make noise." After all, he reasoned, what use is a recording if you can't hear it?

Before long, Edison's recording experiments provided him with the design for a simple device called the phonograph. He created his machine by wrapping tinfoil around a cylin-

Of all his 1,097 patented inventions, the phonograph was Thomas Edison's favorite. He is pictured in the White House with his amazing new device, which he had just demonstrated for President Hayes.

der. A threaded shaft—like a large screw—ran through the cylinder to move it up and down. He then placed a stylus against the device. The stylus moved down the length of the cylinder as the cylinder turned.

Sound was recorded on the cylinder as grooves in the tinfoil. When the stylus came into contact with the grooves, it began to vibrate. These vibrations produced a faint sound. Edison had just created the first successful sound recording and playback device!

While Edison's phonograph was a wonderful invention, it wasn't perfect. Part of the problem was that the tinfoil was cut up by the stylus after just a few playings. And the sound made by Edison's first recording was barely recognizable as a human voice.

Edison spent part of 1876 and 1877 trying to improve his phonograph. A series of small but annoying problems left him frustrated. He stopped his work on the phonograph and took up another project he'll long be remembered for—the electric light bulb.

The Graphophone

Like most good ideas, the phonograph would eventually be noticed by someone willing to try to make it better. In 1881, Alexander Graham Bell—who earlier had invented the telephone—decided that the science of recording sound was worth a closer look. He carefully studied Edison's phonograph and decided to try to improve it.

Bell, along with two friends, worked long hours in his Volta laboratory. They wanted to make a device that not only recorded sound, but also reproduced it in a more lifelike way. The result was a machine called the Graphophone.

The Graphophone looked very much like Edison's phonograph. There were some differences, however. Instead of tinfoil, the new device used cardboard rolls coated with wax. Then a stylus carved grooves in the wax in response to sound vibrations. This made the sound smoother and more lifelike.

Bell's machine was also easier to operate than Edison's phonograph.

Alexander Graham Bell was known for his many inventions. In addition to the telephone, Bell developed the Graphophone, an improved version of Edison's phonograph.

Instead of using a handcrank to turn the cardboard rolls, a foot pedal kept the cylinder turning at a constant speed.

But the Graphophone wasn't perfect either. There was no way to make more than one recording at a time from the original sound. And the wax coating on the cylinders wore out almost as fast as tinfoil.

Berliner and the Record

Most people mistakenly give credit to Thomas Edison for inventing the "record." Although he did contribute, that honor really goes to a man named Emile Berliner.

Berliner spent long hours studying Edison's and Bell's problem of short-lived recordings. Finally, he experimented with a flat disk that looks much like the records that are used today.

Berliner took a sheet of zinc—a sturdy metal—and cut round discs from it. The discs were coated with fat and placed onto a platter, which was then attached to a horn by a series of wheels and pulleys. The entire device was turned with a crank. At the small end of the horn was a stylus that was used to cut grooves into the fat-coated discs.

When someone sang or spoke, the sound caused the horn to vibrate. The stylus at the end of the horn cut grooves in the fat. When the recording was complete, the fat-covered disc was dipped into an acid bath. The acid ate away the fat and left a shiny disc with the recording etched in a thin groove. The groove ran around the outside of the disc in a spiral pattern, like a modern LP.

Berliner used a different stylus—called a "playback" stylus—to play the recording. The sound came out through a horn attached to the playback stylus.

By today's standards, the sound quality was poor. Yet Berliner's records offered a great advantage over previous systems. The zinc disc could be played many times. This invention opened the door for the birth of the recording industry.

This strange-looking device is a Gramophone. It used "records" made of zinc, like those developed by Emile Berliner.

CHAPTER TWO

A NEW INDUSTRY

Music for Everyone

Before Edison, Berliner, and Bell came up with a way to record music, the only way to enjoy music was to hear it live. This was a problem for many people who did not live near the great performing halls of the day.

In the late 1800's, professional concerts were common only to those in the large cities. Travelling to such performances was out of the question for most people. And only the well-to-do could afford tickets to such events.

The invention of the phonograph and other devices opened up the music world to millions of people. As was the case with the invention of the automobile, an entire industry sprang up—literally overnight. People, rich and poor alike, were starved for music. This caused the demand for phonographs and records to skyrocket in the 1890's.

The First Metal Master

Berliner refined his record-making process by recording music on hard rubber. This method was much cheaper than zinc. Although the rubber discs wore out faster than the zinc ones, Berliner then found that he could make many rubber copies from an original metal disc. A metal "master" is still used today for records and compact discs.

In the meantime, Edison's phonograph was continually being improved. The Edison Company had at least 12 different kinds of phonographs for sale. But the problem of making the phonograph's cylinder recordings last more than a few playings was never really solved.

Tone Arms Save the Day

By 1900, many inventors had turned their attention to improving the sound quality of phonographs and recordings. Speaker horns were getting bigger and this placed extra weight on the stylus and record grooves. Records quickly wore out.

Eldridge Johnson of the Victor Company came up with a solution to this problem in 1904. He invented the "tone arm." The tone arm worked by reducing the weight of the speaker horn on the record grooves.

Speaker horns were made bigger and bigger. Some, like the one shown above, were literally room-size.

Johnson's invention helped make phonographs more popular than ever thought possible. His company's profits were nearly $1 million that year alone!

The Victrola

At this point, the phonograph still looked like a bulky "machine." Johnson knew that women—who often helped to make the buying decision—weren't thrilled with the clumsy look. He concluded that the phonograph should look more like a piece of furniture in order to appeal to women. It turned out he was right.

Johnson asked a crew of technicians and cabinetmakers to restyle the phonograph. He wanted to create a beautiful piece of furniture that would be welcome in any family's parlor.

Johnson called the new product the "Victrola." It was a huge success. The Victor Company placed advertisements in magazines like the *Saturday Evening Post*. But word-of-mouth alone soon brought in thousands of orders.

Keep Playing That Song!

As sales of phonographs increased, the demand for records exploded. To get an edge on the competition, the Victor Company paid huge sums of money to sign famous singers to recording contracts. Opera star Enrico Caruso was one of the first to make recordings for them.

By 1914, three companies—Edison, Victor, and Columbia—were selling more than $27 million worth of phonographs a year. And record sales were even greater. In 1919, Americans purchased almost $160 million worth of records!

CHAPTER THREE

NEW & IMPROVED RECORDINGS

Electric Recordings

By this time, consumers were demanding better quality recordings. Companies spent millions of dollars to find ways to improve a record's sound quality. It wasn't enough, anymore, just to hear music on a phonograph. The music had to sound good, too! And the challenge of creating realistic sound is **still** very much an issue for the recording industry.

"Electric recordings" improved the sound quality of records dramatically. This photo shows Dinah Shore recording in 1946.

After years of research, a man named J.P. Maxfield created a system for making better-sounding recordings. He used two new devices—a microphone and an amplifier—to make what he called the "electric recording."

Maxfield's microphone was able to respond to sound waves and turn the sound into weak electrical impulses. The amplifier was another electrical device that took these signals and made them more powerful.

A microphone and amplifier could be hooked up to a speaker to play sound. But Maxfield used this combination to drive a stylus that made permanent recordings.

Maxfield's company, Western Electric, advertised his electric recording system as a breakthrough in sound quality. And, for the most part, they were right.

Electric recordings were far bet-

Because there were often technical problems, two recordings of a single performance were usually made at the same time. This recording session was for Gene Krupa (on the drums) in 1947.

ter than anything else available at the time. But there was still a problem. There was no phonograph available to listeners that was capable of matching the improved quality of these electric recordings.

The 78

In the 1920's, a new kind of record was introduced. It was called a 78, and it quickly became a success.

The 78 got its name from the speed at which it was played on a phonograph. In order for the music to sound just right, the record had to be spun at exactly 78 revolutions, or turns, per minute.

The 78 could hold about four minutes of music or speech. This compared to a maximum of two minutes on the cylinders.

Using Maxfield's recording system, the makers of 78's were able to

The 78 was more rugged than earlier records, and its sound quality was much better.

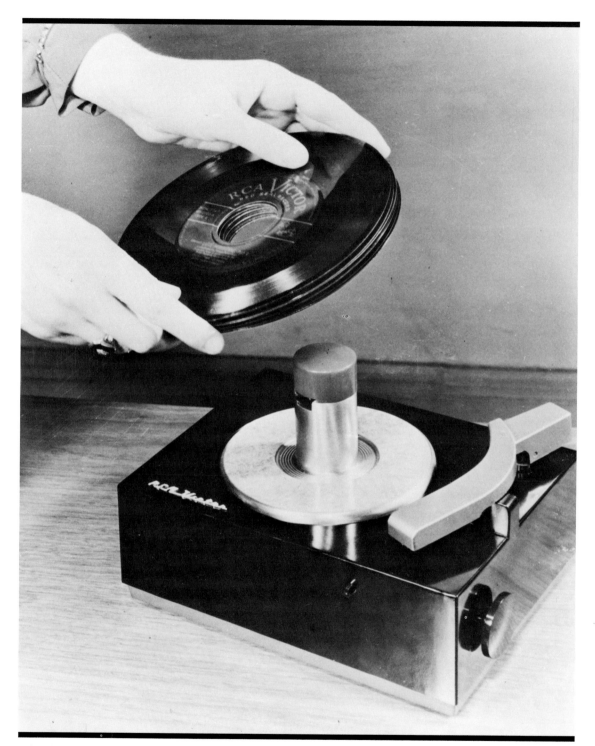

The 45 could only hold a few minutes of music, but its light weight allowed several to be stacked on a spindle like the one shown above. RCA introduced the 45 during the 1950's.

achieve better sound quality than ever before. The record-buying public went wild, and 78's were sold as quickly as they could be made.

The 78 was a major advance over previous types of records, but it did have some serious drawbacks. 78's were easily chipped or broken. Their four- or-five-minute playing time still wasn't enough to satisfy music lovers. Even so, 78's remained the record of choice until the late 1940's.

The LP & the 45

In 1948, Dr. Peter Goldmark of CBS Laboratories (Columbia Records' parent company), invented the 33 1/3 rpm Long Playing Record. The LP, as it was called, was 12 inches in diameter. And LP's could hold more than 25 minutes of music on each side of the disc!

The LP was designed to play at less than half the speed of a 78. This, along with more grooves per inch, helped the LP pack more music on a single disc. And existing phonographs—with a few adjustments—could play both LP's and 78's.

CBS' competitor, RCA, liked the new LP format. But it quickly introduced its own "improvement." This was a 7-inch record that played at 45 revolutions per minute. It had a large hole in the center, which meant it could only be played on special phonographs that RCA also sold. The 45 really wasn't much better than the 78. It, too, could hold only about four minutes of music. But because it was new, it sold well.

Within a short time, almost all record companies—including RCA—offered their music on both LP and 45 formats. By the end of 1950, the 78 rpm record was almost extinct.

CHAPTER FOUR

TAPE RECORDINGS

Making Patterns

At this point, the process for making records was difficult and very slow. There was a need for a system that made the recording process simpler. Besides, records still tended to wear out quickly.

LP's were an improvement over other types of recordings. But the wear and tear of a stylus on a record made most records very noisy after just a few playings.

From the 1920's through the end of World War II, a group of scientists in the United States and Germany worked on a new system for recording sound.

The scientists used a very simple principal as the basis for their experiments. When iron filings are spread on a piece of paper and a magnet is held near them, the filings will move into various patterns when affected by the magnet's charge. The scientists found that paper or plastic tape coated with metallic oxide reacted to an electrical charge.

Metallic oxide is a material that is made up of tiny metal particles. These particles are very sensitive to magnetic charges. When bonded to a reel of tape, the particles could be rearranged by the recording device.

Eventually, recording machines were built to give off magnetic charges in certain patterns. This allowed tape recorders to produce recognizable sounds.

A "Two-headed" Machine

A tape recorder sends signals through a recording "head" that

Magnetic tape changed the recording industry. Recording on tape was better, cheaper, and easier than earlier methods.

Cassette tapes became popular in the 1970's. They allowed people to make recordings just about anywhere!

changes the particles on the tape itself. As more and more of the tape passes the recording head, sound patterns are created. This fact allows magnetic tape to record sound.

A playback head is used to play the tape. The playback head does not give off a charge. That would ruin a recorded tape. Instead, a playback head simply **responds** to the tape as it passes the head. Certain patterns in the tape particles cause the tape player to produce a specific sound.

Because a tape recorder or player uses smooth recording and playback heads, there is very little wear on the tape itself. This gives it an advantage over more fragile records. But the biggest advantage to music lovers is that tape recorders allow them to make their **own** recordings.

By making copies of records and live performances, anyone can put together their favorite selections on a single tape. With records, people have to live with what they get. With tape recorders, they can mix and match songs to suit their tastes.

Takin' it to the Streets

At one time, three types of recording tape formats existed side by side. In the 1960's and 1970's, reel-to-reel, cassettes, and 8-track tapes were all very popular. Their success was mostly due to the fact that they were compact and much less sensitive to movement than records and phonographs. This meant tape players could be taken almost anywhere.

Cassette and 8-track tapes proved to be sturdy enough to be played in automobiles. Automakers had experimented with record players in cars, but the idea "bombed." With the introduction of high quality tape players and prerecorded tapes, music took to the road. And the beach. And just about everywhere else!

By the 1980's, the Sony company of Japan introduced the portable "Walkman" cassette player. It was smaller than a paperback book.

Yet it could reproduce incredible sound quality through lightweight headphones.

The portable cassette player had a huge impact on cassette sales. Suddenly, cassettes were **the** recording system of choice. By 1983 cassettes were outselling records. And in 1988, two cassettes were sold for every record!

CHAPTER FIVE

DIGITAL COMPACT DISCS

Computers Speed Progress

No one would argue that the computer age has changed the world. It seems that computers are everywhere. And ever since the first computer was invented in the 1940's, people have been trying to find a way to make computers, music, and recordings go together.

Progress has been slow. Many important inventions—transistors, microchips, and more—have brought us into the computer age.

While computers have been used in recording equipment for years, the trick was to make computers small and powerful enough to handle the demands of recording and playing music.

In the early 1970's, computers took a giant leap forward. Scientists found a way to squeeze thousands of electronic circuits into a space the size of a person's thumbnail.

This invention—called the integrated circuit, or microchip—opened the door for some amazing things. The microchip helped computers work very fast and take up much less room than ever was imagined.

This was a great stride forward in the computer industry—and in the recording business, as well.

Digital Audio Technology

As computers became more powerful, they were able to analyze music. A computer could "listen" to music and put it into a form that other computers could understand. Such information—or "data"— could be stored on a disc or tape for

The digital compact disc—or CD—uses microscopic pits to store sounds. The CD offers amazing sound quality compared to records and cassettes.

future use. This process was called "digital recording." The music could be "sampled" by a computer and played back with incredible quality.

By the late 1970's, record companies began recording music with computers. This process was called digital audio technology. But there was a problem.

As good as digital audio was, putting music of this quality on a vinyl record seemed like a waste. Record makers searched for a proper way to store the digital music. They needed a system that could be used by people in their homes, not just by computers in laboratories.

Finally a solution was found. In 1984, Sony introduced a new recording method that was right out of the computer age. It was called an optical disc. Today, the optical disc is called a compact disc, or CD.

A CD is about one-third the size of an LP. It has a hole in the middle like an LP, but it's less than 1/20th of an inch high!

In the center of a CD is a shiny layer of aluminum or silver. On either side are two layers of sturdy plastic to protect it from damage. If you hold a CD up to a light, it will reflect the light like a prism.

Compact discs store sound as pits in a track—like footsteps in the sand. Each pit represents a number. This tells the CD player what sound to produce. Each CD has billions of these tiny pits on its surface. They are so small that they can only be seen through a microscope.

Because the pits are so small, they cannot be played by an ordinary phonograph. Instead, a machine—called a CD player—uses a low-powered laser beam to "play" the CD. And unlike a phonograph, a CD player begins reading the "information" on a CD from the inside and continues toward the outside edge of the disc.

Because CD's are "played" with a laser beam, they last far longer than even the best LP or cassette tape. An LP becomes worn with just one playing. It gets worse the more it is played. A CD, on the other hand, doesn't have the problem of friction. That means a CD can be played thousands of times and still sound new.

This videodisc contains both digital sound and video images! The player works just like a regular CD player.

By 1988, CD's were outselling LP's. Some experts even predicted that CD's would make LP's extinct by 1990!

And that's not all. The pits on a CD can also represent words or pictures. Some CD's actually include **both** music and video images. And scientists are now working on a CD system that will store sound, TV pictures, words and computer programs all on the same disc.

CHAPTER SIX

INSIDE THE RECORDING STUDIO

A Team Effort

We owe a great debt to inventors and scientists like Edison, Berliner and others. They have made sound recordings a magical and important part of our lives. But there is another part of the story waiting to be told. Even with the best machines and the latest recording technology, there is more to a recording than meets the eye and ear.

Somewhere between the great inventions and the record store is the part of the recording industry that actually creates the music and manufactures the records, cassettes, and CD's to which people listen.

The basic process for making LP's, 45's, cassettes, and CD's all begins with the production of a master tape. The master—sometimes called the "original"—is recorded in a soundproof room (called a studio) or in a concert hall.

A studio is carefully designed and built to create the the best possible sound for the recording process. On every wall—even the ceiling and floor—is sound-absorbing material that soaks up every echo and other noises that can spoil a good performance.

Inside the studio is a maze of wires, microphones, music stands, recording equipment, and musical instruments. Each has a separate function, but they all work together when the recording session begins.

The person in charge of the studio is the producer. It is the producer's job to make sure that everything is ready for the recording session and that all runs smoothly. The producer is the "boss" of the recording session.

The recording engineer joins the producer before the musicians arrive to check all of the details of the recording. The recording engineer is the link between the producer, the musicians, and the recording equipment. Recording engineers are highly trained to get the right sound on the master tape.

Take One!

The tape machine used by the engineer is specially made to record more than one sound or voice on the tape. Most tape recorders used in the studio can record from four to 32 separate channels, or tracks, on a single tape. This means that dozens of different instruments or vocals can be recorded separately.

The recording engineer can check sound levels while a drummer warms up before the start of a recording session.

Usually, the rhythm section (drums, bass, and guitar) and other instruments are recorded before the vocals. The lead vocalist listens to this recording on headphones to get the proper tempo or pitch as he or she sings. Other vocal parts can be recorded as needed.

Because it is difficult to get everything right on the first try, the producer will ask the musician or singer to make a number of "takes." The best of these is then used in the final recording.

A multi-track recording system can also be used to isolate the sound of certain instruments to get a unique effect.

Many musicians use electronic devices to change the sound of the instruments after they are recorded. A guitar that sounds like a guitar in the studio may be electronically "changed" to sound like a freight train!

Vocals can be treated the same way. A recording engineer can make a weak singer sound as strong as an orchestra by adding an echo effect to the vocal recording.

Mixing Magic

Once the basic recording is made, the recording engineer will play it back. The producer and musicians will listen carefully to the recording. They must decide which performances should be included in the master tape.

The recording engineer can also play the various instruments and vocals in different combinations to get the right arrangement. And, if a musician or singer makes a mistake, his or her performance can be re-recorded until it is perfect, without affecting any of the other tracks.

When everything is right, the recording engineer will blend the tracks. This process is called "mixing." The result of mixing is a master tape that sounds like everyone recorded together, instead of at different times. The recording engineer can still make changes—or "edit"— the tape until everyone is satisfied with the results.

CHAPTER SEVEN

HOW RECORDS ARE MADE

From Lacquer to Master

Once the master tape is finished, a record can be made. Part of the process of making a record begins in the studio.

Technicians create a disc called a master "lacquer" from the master tape right in the studio. The music on the master tape is transferred to the lacquer by a machine called a cutting lathe. The lathe uses a stylus to cut a narrow groove in the soft plastic that coats the lacquer.

The groove is cut in a spiral pattern that moves toward the center of the lacquer. One side of the groove holds the music that was on the left channel of the master tape. The other side contains the music from the right channel of the tape. The louder the sound on the tape, the deeper and wider the groove is cut on the lacquer. During quiet passages, the groove is very shallow and narrow. One lacquer is made for each side of the record.

A computer is used to check the recording as the lacquer is made. The computer guides the cutting lathe, so that the grooves are cut as close together as possible without interfering with each other. This allows more music per side on the lacquer.

If there is a problem with the lacquer, a new copy must be made. This process is repeated until the recording is perfect. When the lacquer is finished, it is shipped to a record manufacturing plant. It is inspected very carefully. If it passes, the lacquer is cleaned and prepared for the next step in the process.

In the 1940's, masters were made at the same time the performance was happening. These recording engineers were inspecting the operation of the cutting lathes.

The lacquer is coated with a thin surface of nickel. When the nickel coating is pulled away from the lacquer, it is called a metal master. Then it is inspected again for defects.

The metal master is a negative copy of the lacquer, similar to a photographic negative. The metal master has ridges where the lacquer had grooves.

From Master to Mother

The metal master is cleaned very carefully. It is plated with another layer of nickel. This layer is removed from the metal master and is called a mother. This copy is positive—with grooves that match the grooves from the lacquer. The mother is cleaned and tested by an expert.

Because the grooves on the mother are so small, a technician must use a microscope to check for any flaws. The mother is played on a highly sensitive device that looks like a large record player. If the grooves are too big or too small, or if there are imperfections, the music will not sound right. The mother will then be rejected. Often the technician can correct the problem, but a new mother will sometimes be required before the record-making process can continue.

If the mother is approved, it is plated several times to create negative copies called stampers. The stampers are used to create the finished records. There is a separate stamper for each side of a record. A hole is punched or drilled in the stamper and the edges are trimmed and sanded. The stamper is measured and inspected and sent to the press room.

Biscuits & Stampers

A record press is a large machine that uses high pressure to make records. There are two different kinds of presses—one each for 45's and LP's—but they both work the same. Some record manufacturers have enough presses to produce tens of thousands of records a day.

Once the stampers have been carefully placed on the press, the process of making the actual record

The metal master is carefully inspected before it is used to make records.

is ready to begin. Two record labels—one for each side—are automatically put on the stampers.

Vinyl is the material from which records are made. This plastic material is heated into a blob, called a biscuit, and is dropped between the stampers.

The stampers slowly squeeze together, pressing the plastic into the correct shape and thickness. Cold water is circulated through the press to harden the disc. A finished record is then carefully removed from the press.

Several records from each pressing session are tested. If the tester hears or sees a problem, the press will be shut down until the problem is corrected. If the record passes this test, it is sent to an inspector.

Record inspectors have the job of taking a final look at the finished record before it is packaged and shipped. Inspectors examine the record for any defects. Their trained eyes look for scratches, crooked labels, warping, or anything else that could mean the record is less than perfect.

Off to the Stores!

Once a record is approved by the inspectors, it is placed into a thin paper sleeve. Another worker places the record into a cardboard jacket. The jacket is also known as the record cover. It is decorated to suit the tastes of the performer and the record company.

The finished product is wrapped in cellophane and boxed with others. The box of records is sealed and sent to the shipping department, where it is labeled. A truck takes it to a huge distribution center. The records are then sold to smaller distributors or directly to record stores. Finally, the records are placed into racks where—hopefully—they are purchased and taken home.

CHAPTER EIGHT

MAKING TAPES AND CD'S

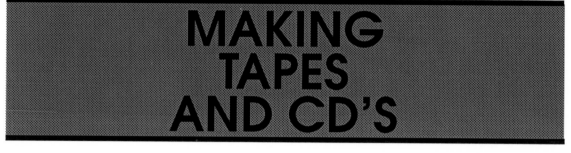

The Running Master

The process of making a cassette tape is very similar to that of a record. One big difference, however, is that cassettes can be recorded almost directly from the master tape.

Instead of a using master lacquer and stampers, cassettes are made from copies of the master tape. When the studio is finished working with the master tape, a copy is made—called the running master—which is sent to a cassette manufacturer.

It takes a number of different parts to make a cassette. Around the manufacturing plant are the various parts of the cassette, waiting for recording and assembly.

In one room is the cassette tape. It is stored on large spools. Plastic cassette shells are boxed and ready for assembly. Near the shells are the clear outer cases that protect the cassettes when they are not in use. Labels and other packaging materials are also stored nearby.

The cassette recording process begins when the running master tape arrives at the manufacturing plant. It is checked very carefully by experts for any problems. Sometimes a magnetic charge will erase part of the master tape and cause "drop-outs." Very cold or hot temperatures or poor handling can also ruin a master tape—or any tape recording, for that matter.

Hard-working Slaves

If the master tape is approved, it is sent to a special "clean room" for "tailoring." The tape is fastened

Magnetic tape is loaded into a shell to create a cassette.

together at both ends to form a loop. The tape can then be played endlessly without stopping. The running master is loaded into a master machine that is electronically linked to dozens of tape recorders, called "slaves."

The slaves have one purpose: to make recordings of the master onto standard cassette tape. The slaves are automated, so that when the running master gets to the end of the recording, the slave inserts blank tape to separate one complete recording from another.

After about 40 recordings of the running master are made, a technician collects the tapes—called "pancakes"—and listens to the recordings.

If the pancakes are OK, they are split up into separate recordings. A blank leader is attached to the beginning and end of each recording, and the tapes are loaded into the shells. The recording is now a cassette.

The cassettes are tested a final time, and are put into cases, wrapped, boxed and shipped to warehouses and record stores.

Making CD's: No Dust Allowed

The making of CD's could be summed up in one word: clean. The reason is simple, but important.

Music is stored on CD's in microscopic pits. These pits are so small that billions will fit on a single CD. Because each pit is about 1/20th of the size of a speck of dust, even the smallest dust particle can damage the quality of a CD.

The people who make CD's wear the same kind of protective clothing as doctors in an operating room. And anyone who enters a CD manufacturing room must take an "air shower" to remove dust and other small materials from their bodies.

The Master

A CD is generally made from the same master tape used for the cassette and record version of a recording. Once the master is complete, a copy is sent to the CD manufacturing plant, where it is tested thoroughly by humans and computers. Even the smallest error means the

Although great care must be taken while making CD's, the results are worth it—CD sound is "awesome!"

master tape is returned to the studio and a replacement must be made.

The digital information on the master tape must be transferred to a master CD. This master CD is made of a special round glass plate. The glass is highly polished until it is perfectly flat and smooth. Then the plate is tested by a laser.

Fathers, Mothers, & Sons

If the plate passes inspection, it is coated with a material called "photoresist." Once the glass plate is properly prepared, it goes into another clean room where it is no longer touched by humans. The plate is placed on a cutting lathe. A powerful cutting laser beam etches pits into the glass in a very precise pattern. The cutting laser receives its signals from the master tape. A smaller laser helps to focus and track the cutting laser along its path.

The glass plate rotates at 200 rpm or faster during this process. After the pits have been burned in by the cutting laser, the plate—now called a master disc—moves to a machine that washes it in a special developing solution. This mixture helps "burn-in" the pits to the proper depth.

The master disc is plated with silver. This creates a disc called the "father." It is mirror image of the master disc. The father is used to make a number of "mothers" and "sons" which are used as stampers.

If this process sounds familiar, it should be. The process for making CD's and LP's is fairly similar once the master disc is made.

The Finishing Touches

The stampers are sent to a pressing machine. There, a glob of plastic is injected between the stampers and is pressed into the shape of a CD. The discs are checked by another laser for any imperfections. Those that pass are given a reflective coating of aluminum, silver, or gold. The final step is to seal the CD with a thin layer of plastic. After this coat dries, the label is printed directly on the CD with a process called "silk-screening."

The discs can now be touched

and inspected a final time. They are played at high speed and checked for any imperfections in the music or the CD itself.

The CD's are then packaged in a plastic "jewel box," boxed and shipped to distribution centers across the world.

With CD's, it's now possible to have nearly "concert hall sound" right in your living room!

CHAPTER NINE

MIRACLES FOR EVERYONE

Over the past 125 years, we have become used to miracles. Sound recording, once an unthinkable impossibility, is a common, familiar part of our lives. What was once an outrageous challenge is now reality. Recordings are instantly accessible for almost everyone. At the beach, we slip a cassette into a portable stereo and create an instant rock concert. In our living rooms, Beethoven's majestic symphonies are stored on a small stack of compact discs.

In the studio, a single musician can play and record the equivalent of an entire orchestra with a lightweight electronic keyboard. A composer can type musical notes onto a computer screen, just as a secretary would type words on paper with a typewriter.

The sound of a piano can be recorded and stored on a microchip the size of a postage stamp. When it is played back—on an electronic keyboard that costs less than $300—not even an expert can tell it from the sound of a real piano.

And tomorrow? Who knows what the limits are?

On the Drawing Board

Within the next few years we will see amazing ideas become reality.

Portable computers will become small enough to carry in a shirt pocket. Musicians will be able to compose and record their music anywhere. They will be able to put themselves in the middle of an orchestra by popping a tiny diskette into their computer.

Erasable compact discs that can be recorded in your home will become common.

A laser phonograph will eliminate record wear. Because nothing but a small laser beam will touch the record, the sound quality will be better than ever.

Some inventors think that even musicians will become obsolete. Each household will be able to ask a computer to create music with the touch of a single button. The computer will be able to "think" like a composer. And it will play music suited to a person's individual tastes.

The list of ideas goes on and on. What seemed impossible just a few years ago is now real. And tomorrow's inventions will have the same effect on listeners as Thomas Edison's phonograph had on a doubtful group of men in 1877.

○ ○ ○

It is 1877. A group of men recoil in shock at the scratchy sound of a man's voice coming from Thomas Edison's phonograph.

It is 1988.

A young girl walks into a department store. She spots an electronic keyboard on display. Her fingers dance across the keys, and the sound of an entire orchestra surrounds her. She presses a small button on the keyboard and the sound changes to the gruff barking of a dog. She laughs and presses another button. The sound changes again, this time to a pipe organ. She plays a few more notes, grows bored, and leaves.

Times have changed.

GLOSSARY

amplifier—an electrical device that takes weak electrical signals and makes them stronger.

biscuit—a blob of molten vinyl compressed under high pressure into records or CD's.

compact disc (CD)—a thin, round disc that contains music or other sounds in digital form. A CD is played, or "read," by a laser beam.

digital recording—a method of recording in which sound is converted to electronic bits. The bits are recorded onto magnetic tape and then used to create CD's and other digital recordings.

electrical impulse—a small movement of electricity.

integrated circuit—a tiny electronic "chip" containing many smaller circuits (or switches).

lacquer—a master record used to make other records in the manufacturing process.

magnetic tape—a thin plastic material coated with a metallic oxide, which is sensitive to an electrical charge. It is commonly used for making recordings and cassettes.

master tape—the tape that is used to record a performance. The master tape is used as the source for recordings on cassettes, records, and CD's.

metal master—the metal disc that is used to create a "mother" disc. It is a negative image of a record, with ridges instead of grooves.

microphone—a device used to change sound into electrical impulses that are used in recording.

mixing—blending the different sounds or "tracks" of a recording.

"mother"—a metal disc that is used to create the stampers that press the records.

producer—the person in charge of the studio during a recording session.

rpm—revolutions per minute. A 45 record makes 45 complete revolutions per minute.

speaker—a paper or plastic cone that moves in response to electrical impulses. These movements create sound waves.

stamper—a perfect copy of the "mother" that is used to press grooves into records.

stylus—the "needle" on a record player. The stylus tracks along the groove in a record. Tiny ridges along the groove make the stylus vibrate. These vibrations are turned into electrical signals, which produce sound when amplified.

tape recorder—a device that uses small electrical charges to leave a pattern on magnetic tape. The recording head creates the patterns, while the playback head turns the patterns into sound.

tone arm—an arm that pivots, allowing the needle, or stylus, to move along the groove in a record.

INDEX